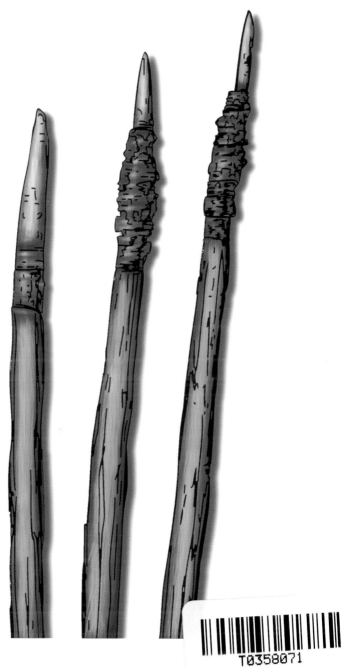

1

T0358071

The First Peoples used stone for all their tools.

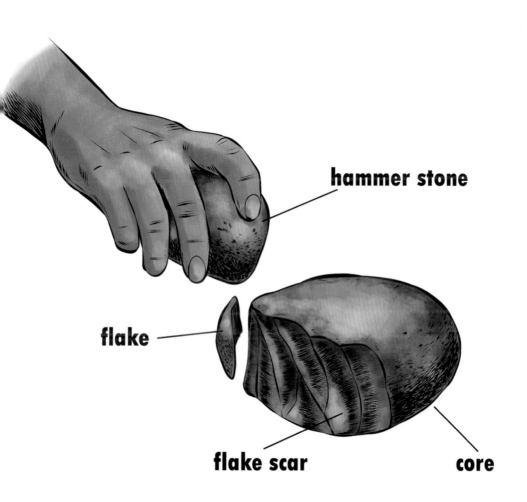

hammer stone

flake

flake scar

core

3

Stone flakes were hit off. The flakes were very sharp.

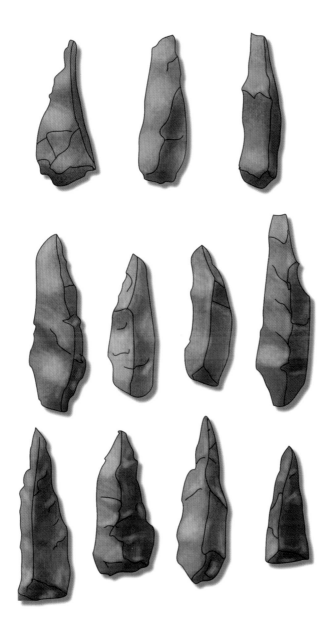

5

The edge of the stone was sharp. The tool could cut skins.

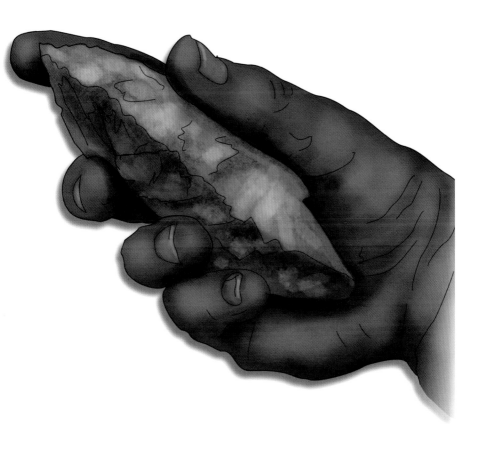

These are heavy clubs. These are weapons. These clubs were made from wood. The words for these clubs are waddys or nulla nullas.

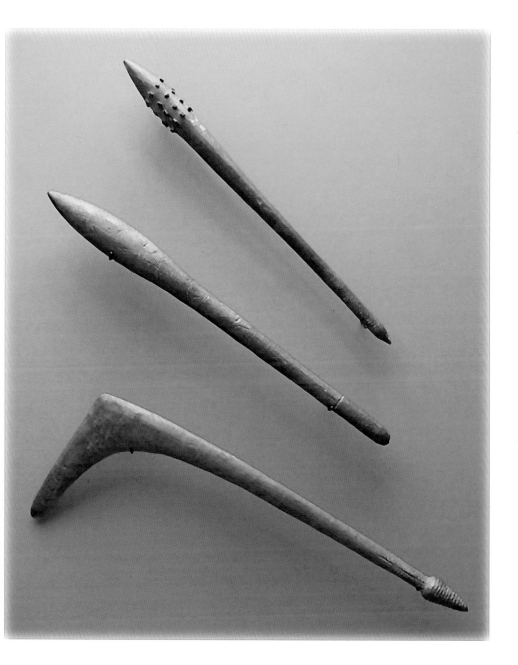

9

The man has a club and shield.
He is ready for battle.

11

The tip of the spear was a sharp stone. The stone tip was tied to the spear.

13

Axes were made from large flat stones.

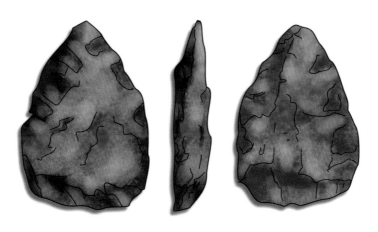

15

These were cutting stones.

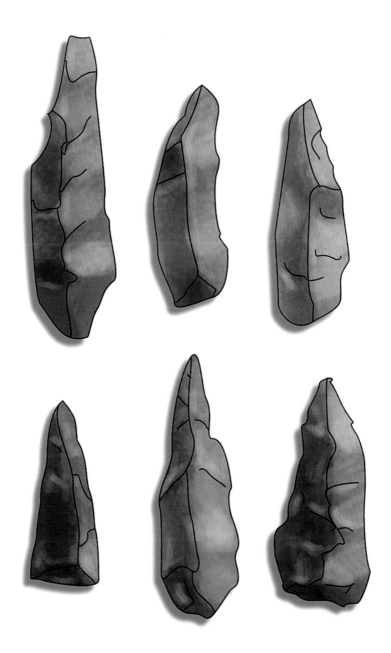

17

These are all axe heads.

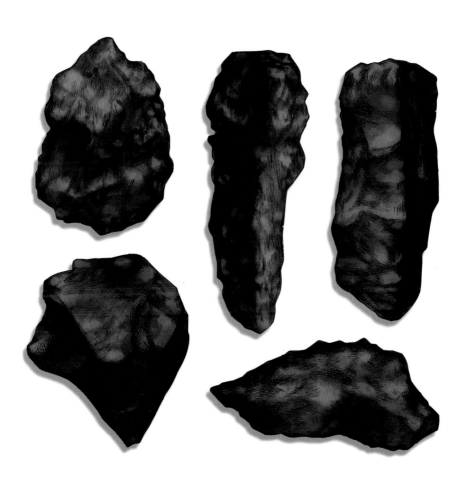

A sharp knife was made with these stones.

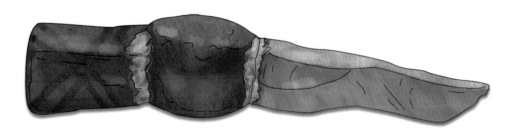

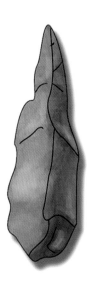

21

The tips of the spears were jagged.

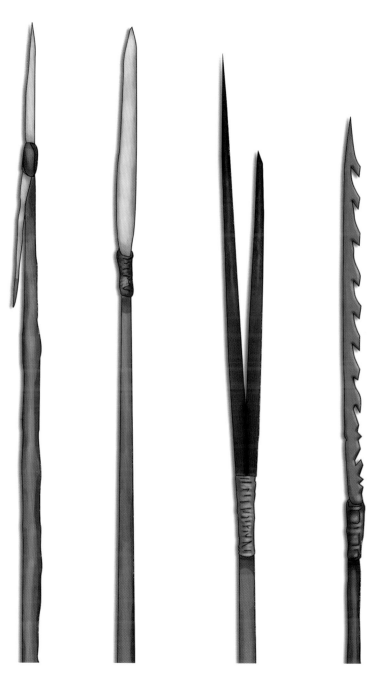

23

Word bank

axes	fur
string	tied
skins	cutting
animal	heads
sharp	knife
edge	jagged
tools	shield
stone	battle
hammer	weapon
flake	club
spear	
straight	